To Kai and Mila,
you don't know what Bitcoin is yet, but you will in time.

This Bitcoin Wallet is For

....

Personal Message

....
....
....
....
....
....
....
....
....
....
....
....
....

This Book is From

....

MY FIRST BITCOIN

A BITCOIN WALLET AND INFO GIFT BOOK

CREATED BY MITCH PERRY

Contents

About this book	1
What is Bitcoin?	3
How are bitcoins created?	4
Bitcoin Halving	7
Bitcoin Halving Chart	8
Who created Bitcoin?	9
Bitcoin is Slow	11
Lightning Network	13
Obtaining Bitcoin	15
Storing Bitcoin	16
Which Bitcoin Wallet?	17
Create my wallet	19
Restore my wallet	21
Sending and Receiving	22
Interesting Bitcoin Facts	25
Wallet Seed Pages	27-48

About this book

This book is designed to be your comprehensive introduction to the world of Bitcoin. My goal for this book is to try provide a non-technical explanation about what Bitcoin is, its creation and most importantly how to safely store bitcoin.

This book also includes a unique feature that sets it apart from other books on the topic - it's a giftable bitcoin wallet!

The wallet section at the back of the book allows you to securely store your bitcoin, making it a great keepsake gift for a newborn's birth, a birthday or any other special occasion.

To gift this book as well as a bitcoin wallet, create a bitcoin wallet and write down the 12-24 seed word phrase in the wallet section. Once you've sent a small amount of bitcoin to the wallet, you can gift someone this book. This is a great gift idea for someone who is new to Bitcoin or wants to learn more.

The book includes a dedicated section on bitcoin wallets, which covers everything from wallet creation and restoration to sending and receiving bitcoin transactions. This is also a great resource for anyone looking to learn about storing their bitcoin safely and securely.

Remember, as the saying goes, "not your keys, not your coins!"

"History has shown that governments will inevitably succumb to the temptation of inflating the money supply."

Saifedean Ammous
Author, The Bitcoin Standard.

What is Bitcoin?

Bitcoin (BTC) is a borderless digital currency that lives on the internet. Bitcoin is hard money that cannot be controlled by any one person or group. It's created and distributed amongst people around the world everyday.

The payments between the users do not require a third-party to be involved; transactions take place directly between the individuals using bitcoin.

The Bitcoin network also known as 'blockchain' records every transaction. It's similar to a bank ledger. However, unlike bank ledgers, anyone can view it, and it's a permanent record of every transaction that has taken place.

Each transaction is added to a 'block'. This block contains a list of other transactions. The users connected to the Bitcoin network all have a copy of the entire blockchain. This is a distributed ledger and all users are verifying these transactions.

The verified block is linked to a block which is linked to another block, and so on, creating a series of blocks chained together, which serves as a record of all transactions that have been verified by all users on the network, hence the word 'blockchain'.

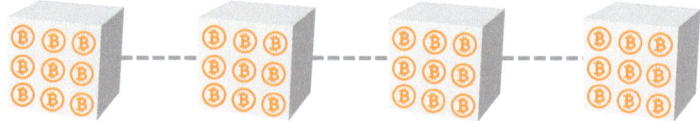

How are bitcoins Created?

Bitcoins are created by a process called "mining" which involves users connecting to the Bitcoin network to process and verify user transactions. By doing so, they are maintaining the security of the Bitcoin blockchain.

The miners are expending a certain amount of computational effort to process these bitcoin transactions. They are trying to solve a complex mathematical puzzle in order to verify the authenticity of a transaction. When they solve this puzzle, the user or group of users mining as an incentive for their work are issued with newly generated bitcoins. Specifically, each time a miner successfully adds a new block to the blockchain, they are granted a certain amount of bitcoins as a reward.

This is the reward for the miners for maintaining the Bitcoin blockchain. The process takes place every time a block has been solved, which is roughly every ten minutes. The end result of each blockchain verification process is called 'proof of work' (PoW) and it provides a secure and decentralized way of verifying transactions without relying on a central authority.

Think of proof of work like when you go to your job you expend a certain amount of energy to complete your work. You are then rewarded for this work with a payment for your services. It is very similar to the way the Bitcoin system works.

Bitcoin's blockchain is essentially one giant database of transactions. Its a database that cannot be altered. The more computing power in the network, the more secure and resistant to attack it becomes.

The strength of Bitcoin's network has grown exponentially since it's creation and is constantly growing. A hacker would need to control 51% of Bitcoin's network in order to cause disruption.

This would require great amounts of computing power and the attacker would not be receiving the blockchain mining rewards. The attacker would benefit more financially from participating in the mining instead of trying to attack it.

There will only ever be 21 million bitcoins created. This is digital money that cannot be inflated or manipulated. Such as currencies attached to a country or system of government.

Just like how our dollar can be divided into smaller amounts, one bitcoin can be divided into up to eight decimal places, with smaller units called satoshis or sats.

Bitcoin (BTC)	Satoshis
1.00000000	100,000,000
0.10000000	10,000,000
0.01000000	1,000,000
0.00100000	100,000
0.00010000	10,000
0.00001000	1000
0.00000100	100
0.00000010	10
0.00000001	1

"The current financial system runs on printed cash. They are screwing with the money and it's hurting you and your family. That's why people buy bitcoin."

Jason A. Williams
Author, Bitcoin: Hard Money You Can't F*ck With.

Bitcoin Halving

Approximately every four years, the reward for mining Bitcoin is cut in half. These "halvings" reduce the rate at which new bitcoins are created. This event is hard-coded into the Bitcoin software and is designed to control the issuance of new bitcoins.

When Bitcoin was created in 2009, the reward was set at 50 bitcoins. In the first halving in 2012, the reward was reduced to 25 bitcoins per block. The second halving took place in 2016, reducing the reward to 12.5 bitcoins per block. The most recent halving occurred in 2020, cutting the reward to 6.25 bitcoins per block.

The halving process continues until the maximum supply of 21 million bitcoins is reached, which is expected to happen around the year 2140. After that point, no new bitcoins will be created through mining rewards. Miners will be paid in transaction fees once the mining end date has been reached.

The halving events are significant because they impact the rate at which new bitcoins enter circulation. By reducing the block reward, halvings create scarcity and can have an effect on the supply and demand dynamics of Bitcoin.

This innovative new concept subsequently transforms Bitcoin into a rare and invaluable form of digital currency.

Bitcoin Halving Chart

By the year 2032, the mining reward will only be (50 halved 6 times) 0.78125 of a bitcoin, and by the year 2044, the reward will then be (50 halved 9 times) 0.09765625 of a bitcoin.

The below chart shows the halving process.

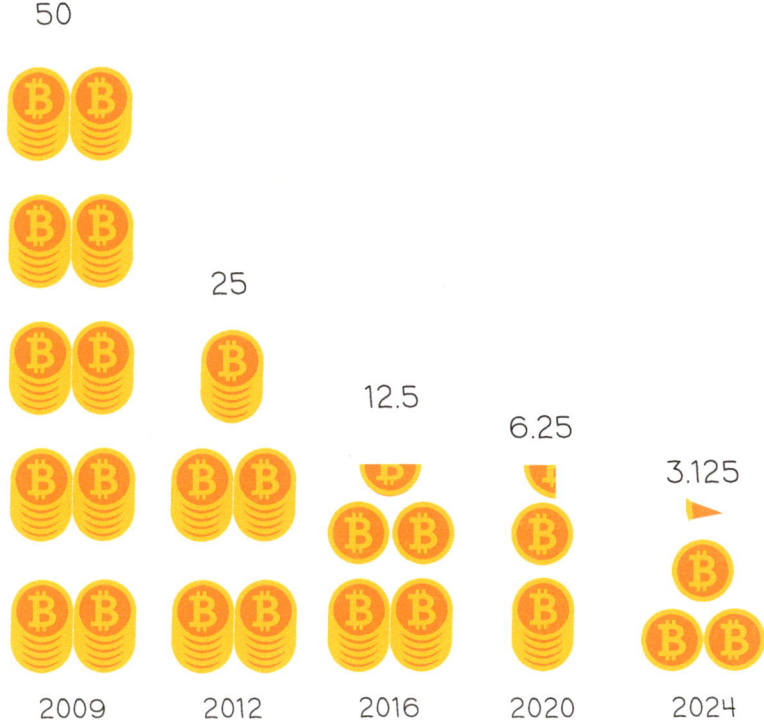

Who Created Bitcoin?

In October 2008, a white paper was published on a cryptography mailing list describing a digital currency. titled "Bitcoin: A Peer-to-Peer Electronic Cash System".

The user who posted this went by the name of Satoshi Nakamoto. Nakamoto stated that work on the writing of the code for Bitcoin began in 2007 and on August 18, 2008, the domain name bitcoin.org was registered.

On January 9, 2009, the Bitcoin network went live and the first block was mined by Satoshi Nakamoto. The reward for this block was 50 bitcoins.

Nakamoto continued to work on the Bitcoin software until mid-2010 and communicated with the Bitcoin community through online forums and emails. Satoshi Nakamoto is a pseudonym, and the true identity of the person or people behind it remains a mystery. It is unclear whether Satoshi Nakamoto is a single person or a group of individuals.

To this day, nobody knows the true identity of Satoshi Nakamoto and the anonymous user has not been heard from since. Over the years, numerous individuals have been suspected of being Nakamoto, but no conclusive evidence has emerged and nobody has ever been able to find out exactly who Satoshi Nakamoto is.

During 2019, Facebook announced they were developing their own cryptocurrency called Libra and it was designed to be used around the world.

Mark Zuckerberg, the CEO of Facebook, testified before the United States Congress in October 2019 to discuss the Libra project. Zuckerberg received backlash from Congress; they were worried that Libra could be a threat to currencies like the US dollar. Regulators then shut down the project.

This could be another reason why Nakamoto maintained his or her anonymity, especially during the early years of Bitcoin's development. If Nakamoto introduced Bitcoin as a public company or a start up, it could of been shut down before it even began. Instead, Bitcoin was developed as an open-source project over the internet.

Satoshi Nakamoto has given the world something special, and Bitcoin's blockchain heartbeat continues to beat without its creator; it lives and breathes on the internet.

Bitcoin is Slow

Bitcoin's transaction speed is often criticized and can be considered slow compared to traditional payment systems such as Visa, Mastercard or even other cryptocurrencies.

The time it takes for a Bitcoin transaction to be confirmed depends on several factors, including network congestion, transaction fees, and the priority assigned to the transaction.

A slow transaction may take place when the fee attached is too low when the network is highly congested. Transactions with a higher fee paid to the miners take priority causing a lower fee transaction to take longer to process.

In general, Bitcoin transactions are considered confirmed after receiving multiple confirmations, which typically takes about 10 minutes on average. However, during periods of high network congestion, it can take longer for transactions to be processed.

Bitcoin may be slower in terms of transaction speeds, but it holds value due to its robust security. The network effect it has built over time, being the most used and accepted cryptocurrency and its decentralized nature.

In the end, Bitcoin's transaction speed limitation depends on specific use cases for the individual.

"Right. Otherwise we couldn't have a finite limit of 21 million coins, because there would always need to be some minimum reward for generating. In a few decades when the reward gets too small, the transaction fee will become the main compensation for nodes. I'm sure that in 20 years there will either be very large transaction volume or no volume."

Satoshi Nakamoto
February 14, 2010 bitcointalk.org

Lightning Network

To address the issue of transaction speeds, various solutions have been proposed and implemented.

Segwit (Segregated Witness) was implemented in the Bitcoin network in 2017 as a protocol upgrade which increased the number of transactions that can be included in each block.

Another solution is the Lightning Network, a layer-two scaling solution built on top of the Bitcoin blockchain.

The Lightning Network enables faster and cheaper transactions by creating payment channels between users, allowing them to conduct transactions off-chain which is then settled on the Bitcoin network later.

Using the Lightning Network side of Bitcoin, you can create a special payment channel directly between you and your friend. It's like creating a secret tunnel just between the two of you.

Say you and your friend both put 1 Bitcoin into this special tunnel. Now you can send small amounts of Bitcoin to each other without telling the whole Bitcoin network about it.

It's like passing notes back and forth in class without the teacher or your peers knowing.

Every time you pass a note, the amounts of Bitcoin in the tunnel get adjusted. If you owe your friend some money, the amount of Bitcoin you have goes down, and the amount your friend has goes up.

The best part is that you don't have to wait for the whole Bitcoin network to confirm every transaction. You can just keep passing notes as much as you want, and it happens really fast!

Once you're done with your transactions, you can close the tunnel, and the final amounts get settled on the Bitcoin network.

Purchasing goods and services with bitcoin using The Lightning solution significantly reduces costs and makes for instant transactions.

Obtaining Bitcoin

There are several ways to obtain bitcoin:

<u>Bitcoin Exchanges:</u> The most popular way is to purchase bitcoin via an online cryptocurrency exchange. These exchanges allow you to purchase Bitcoin using currency (such as AUD, USD, EUR, GBP, etc.)

Exchanges will charge fees for purchasing bitcoin this is how they make money from people buying and selling, each exchange charges different fee amounts. Never leave your bitcoin on an exchange long term remember, not your keys not your coins!

<u>Bitcoin ATMs:</u> Bitcoin ATMs are machines that allow you to buy Bitcoin using cash. They are becoming more popular and can be found in various locations worldwide.

<u>Peer-to-Peer:</u> Users can buy and sell Bitcoin directly from other individuals without the need for an intermediary.

<u>Bitcoin Mining:</u> Bitcoin mining is the process of verifying transactions and adding them to the blockchain. Miners are rewarded with newly minted Bitcoin as an incentive for their work.

<u>Bitcoin as Payment:</u> More and more merchants are accepting Bitcoin as a form of payment. You can use Bitcoin to purchase goods and services from these merchants.

Storing Bitcoin

Just like you would keep your cash in a physical wallet, you can keep your bitcoin in a software-based wallet application.

Bitcoin software wallets are apps that generate and store keys used to send and receive your bitcoin transactions.

You can use a phone application or a computer application to store and manage your bitcoin.

Wallets are backed up by storing a 12-24 word recovery phrase during the initial setup of your bitcoin software wallet.

Consider physically writing the 12-24 words down in order, because if your computer gets attacked by a virus, any keys stored in your computer's files might be at risk.

Most people are probably storing their Bitcoin or cryptocurrency on an exchange, but there is a risk that the exchange could be hacked or fail. This has happened far too often.

If you have your bitcoin on an exchange, technically the exchange owns your bitcoin. If you want to hold your bitcoin long term, it's best to have a personal wallet that you own.

Exchanges come and go, but Bitcoin is here to stay.

Which Bitcoin Wallet?

Blockstream Green

Blockstream Green is an open-source easy-to-use Bitcoin software wallet, It's available on Android, IOS and desktop computers to download.

Jaxx Liberty

Jaxx Liberty securely supports loads of cryptocurrencies and is available for Android, iOS, Mac OSX, Windows, Linux, and also has a Google Chrome extension.

Exodus

An ideal choice for beginners and supports multiple cryptocurrencies. You can download it on Android, iOS and desktop computers.

Hardware Wallets

Software wallets are free to use and setup, while hardware wallets require the physical device to be able to send and receive.

If you are interested in hardware wallets check out ledger.com or trezor.io

"Finally, fiat currencies, while only a relatively recent historical invention, have proven to be prone to constant increases in supply. Nation-states have shown a persistent proclivity to inflate their money supply to solve short-term political problems. The inflationary tendencies of governments across the world leave the owner of a fiat currency with the likelihood that their savings will diminish in value over time."

Vijay Boyapati, Author,
The Bullish Case for Bitcoin.

Create my wallet

To create a wallet you can follow these steps:

1 - Pick a software wallet.

2 - Download the application on your smartphone or computer.

3 - Once installed, open and choose create new wallet.

4 - Some software wallets allow you to pick either 12 or 24 words for your recovery phrase.

5 - Write these words down in order into the My Seed Words section of this book.

6 - Some wallets will ask you to check the backup with words assigned to the numbers so make sure that you have written these down in the correct order.

The software wallet applications will ask for a password or a PIN number to set up so you can use that to log in to your wallet once it has been successfully restored.

Please note that the seed words are always in lowercase.

"Bitcoin is a swarm of cyber hornets serving the goddess of wisdom, feeding on the fire of truth, exponentially growing ever smarter, faster, and stronger behind a wall of encrypted energy."

Michael J. Saylor
Co-founder of MicroStrategy.

Restore my wallet

Restore your wallet by following these steps:

1 - Pick a software wallet that you would like to restore your bitcoin on.

2 - Download the application on your smartphone or computer.

3 - Once opened, there will be a restore or import wallet section within the application.

4. - Upon choosing restore or import wallet, you will see the password recovery phrase section. This will be 12 or 24 words.

5 - Enter your entire seed phrase correctly and in order then hit restore or import.

6 - You will now have access to your bitcoin.

The software wallet applications will ask for a password or a PIN number to set up so you can use that to log in to your wallet once it has been successfully restored.

Please note that the seed words are always in lowercase.

Sending and Receiving

Bitcoin sending and receiving refers to the process of transferring ownership of bitcoins between two parties.

When a sender initiates a Bitcoin transaction, they create a message that contains the recipient's Bitcoin address, the amount of bitcoin being sent, and a digital signature. This message is then broadcast to the Bitcoin network, where it is verified and added to a block of transactions.

Once the transaction is confirmed by the network, the recipient can see the newly received bitcoins in their wallet. They can then spend or transfer the bitcoins by repeating the process.

A bitcoin wallet address contains a string of numbers and letters that looks something like this.

1A1zP1eP5QGefi2DMPTfTL5SLmv7DivfNa

This is the genesis address owned by Satoshi; it received the first bitcoins ever mined. The 50 bitcoins mined are still there.

Over the years, other Bitcoin users have sent their own bitcoins or sats to this address in honor to Satoshi. Currently this address has 72.60631333 BTC, worth (at the time of writing) $2,051,447 US Dollars.

To send bitcoin or sats, a user would copy and paste the address or scan the address using their phone from a QR code provided within the wallet.

Bitcoin Address

3ASeaArDpSqj5DfNWp5XDqJzVUKWrQ9gxE

When you select send, you would enter the Bitcoin address and amount of bitcoin or sats you would like to send. There is usually a minimum send amount and also a small network fee.

Each time you select receive, the Bitcoin address will change each time; if you were sent bitcoin or sats to an old address that you generated you will still receive your bitcoin.

It's important to note that Bitcoin transactions are irreversible, so it's essential to ensure that the transaction details are accurate before sending.

You can view bitcoin wallet transactions on the blockchain explorer.

www.blockchain.com/explorer/assets/btc

"Trust the code and math that is bitcoin, not the human beings"

Anonymous

Interesting Bitcoin Facts

- Approximately 20% of Bitcoin is lost forever. Due to user error from lost wallets, people passing away, forgotten passwords and incorrect transactions.

- The first commercial Bitcoin transaction was for 2 pizzas which cost 10,000 BTC which is now worth (at the time of writing) $294,128,000 US Dollars.

- Miners will create the last bitcoin in 2140.

- On September 2021, President Nayib Bukele announced that Bitcoin would become legal tender in El Salvador along side the U.S. dollar. Making it the first country to accept Bitcoin for goods and services.

- Bitcoin has been used as a hedge against inflation and as a store of value in countries experiencing economic instability or currency devaluation.

Interesting Bitcoin Facts

- Bitcoin transactions are pseudonymous, meaning that while the transactions are recorded on the blockchain, the identities of the individuals involved are not directly revealed.

- Vancouver, Canada was the first city in the world to have a bitcoin ATM.

- Bitcoin has faced criticism for its association with illegal activities due to its perceived anonymity. However, it is important to note that Bitcoin transactions are traceable, and law enforcement agencies have developed techniques to track illicit use.

- Companies such as Tesla, MicroStrategy, and Square have invested significant sums of money into Bitcoin, signaling institutional adoption.

- The Bitcoin network has never been hacked.

Within this segment of the book, you'll discover a dedicated section consisting of ten pages, specifically designed for you to personalise your wallet with information about your first Bitcoin.

There are also ten pages included for the 12-24 seed word phrase.

Following the Create My Wallet or Restore My Wallet pages, this next part of the book you want to keep private and secure as it will be where you write or view your wallet seed words.

If anyone has access to your wallet seed words they can access your bitcoin.

Wallet Name

....

Total Bitcoin In My Wallet

....

Current Bitcoin Price

....

Amount Of Money Spent

....

Date Purchased

....

My Seed Words

1. ....
2. ....
3. ....
4. ....
5. ....
6. ....
7. ....
8. ....
9. ....
10. ....
11. ....
12. ....
13. ....
14. ....
15. ....
16. ....
17. ....
18. ....
19. ....
20. ....
21. ....
22. ....
23. ....
24. ....

....

Wallet Name

....

Total Bitcoin In My Wallet

....

Current Bitcoin Price

....

Amount Of Money Spent

....

Date Purchased

....

My Seed Words

1. ....
2. ....
3. ....
4. ....
5. ....
6. ....
7. ....
8. ....
9. ....
10. ....
11. ....
12. ....
13. ....
14. ....
15. ....
16. ....
17. ....
18. ....
19. ....
20. ....
21. ....
22. ....
23. ....
24. ....

....

Wallet Name

....

Total Bitcoin In My Wallet

....

Current Bitcoin Price

....

Amount Of Money Spent

....

Date Purchased

....

My Seed Words

1. ....
2. ....
3. ....
4. ....
5. ....
6. ....
7. ....
8. ....
9. ....
10. ....
11. ....
12. ....
13. ....
14. ....
15. ....
16. ....
17. ....
18. ....
19. ....
20. ....
21. ....
22. ....
23. ....
24. ....

....

Wallet Name

....

Total Bitcoin In My Wallet

....

Current Bitcoin Price

....

Amount Of Money Spent

....

Date Purchased

....

My Seed Words

1. ....
2. ....
3. ....
4. ....
5. ....
6. ....
7. ....
8. ....
9. ....
10. ....
11. ....
12. ....
13. ....
14. ....
15. ....
16. ....
17. ....
18. ....
19. ....
20. ....
21. ....
22. ....
23. ....
24. ....

....

Wallet Name

....

Total Bitcoin In My Wallet

....

Current Bitcoin Price

....

Amount Of Money Spent

....

Date Purchased

....

My Seed Words

1. ....
2. ....
3. ....
4. ....
5. ....
6. ....
7. ....
8. ....
9. ....
10. ....
11. ....
12. ....
13. ....
14. ....
15. ....
16. ....
17. ....
18. ....
19. ....
20. ....
21. ....
22. ....
23. ....
24. ....

....

Wallet Name

....

Total Bitcoin In My Wallet

....

Current Bitcoin Price

....

Amount Of Money Spent

....

Date Purchased

....

My Seed Words

1. ....
2. ....
3. ....
4. ....
5. ....
6. ....
7. ....
8. ....
9. ....
10. ....
11. ....
12. ....

13. ....
14. ....
15. ....
16. ....
17. ....
18. ....
19. ....
20. ....
21. ....
22. ....
23. ....
24. ....

....

Wallet Name

....

Total Bitcoin In My Wallet

....

Current Bitcoin Price

....

Amount Of Money Spent

....

Date Purchased

....

My Seed Words

1. ....
2. ....
3. ....
4. ....
5. ....
6. ....
7. ....
8. ....
9. ....
10. ....
11. ....
12. ....
13. ....
14. ....
15. ....
16. ....
17. ....
18. ....
19. ....
20. ....
21. ....
22. ....
23. ....
24. ....

....

Wallet Name

....

Total Bitcoin In My Wallet

....

Current Bitcoin Price

....

Amount Of Money Spent

....

Date Purchased

....

My Seed Words

1. ....
2. ....
3. ....
4. ....
5. ....
6. ....
7. ....
8. ....
9. ....
10. ....
11. ....
12. ....
13. ....
14. ....
15. ....
16. ....
17. ....
18. ....
19. ....
20. ....
21. ....
22. ....
23. ....
24. ....

....

Wallet Name

....

Total Bitcoin In My Wallet

....

Current Bitcoin Price

....

Amount Of Money Spent

....

Date Purchased

....

My Seed Words

1. ....
2. ....
3. ....
4. ....
5. ....
6. ....
7. ....
8. ....
9. ....
10. ....
11. ....
12. ....
13. ....
14. ....
15. ....
16. ....
17. ....
18. ....
19. ....
20. ....
21. ....
22. ....
23. ....
24. ....

....

Wallet Name

....

Total Bitcoin In My Wallet

....

Current Bitcoin Price

....

Amount Of Money Spent

....

Date Purchased

....

My Seed Words

1. ....
2. ....
3. ....
4. ....
5. ....
6. ....
7. ....
8. ....
9. ....
10. ....
11. ....
12. ....
13. ....
14. ....
15. ....
16. ....
17. ....
18. ....
19. ....
20. ....
21. ....
22. ....
23. ....
24. ....

....

Acknowledgements

To my amazing wife Charlotte, for giving me ideas, reading the early drafts of this book and your incredible support as I created it. Our kids will have a bright Bitcoin future. Thank you as always.

To my mother, Karen, and my father, John. Throughout the years I have explained the concept of Bitcoin to you. I hope that this little book does the job.

Thank you to my good friends Adam Inder and Robert Browning for reviewing the initial drafts, providing advice and making edits.

Thank you to Saifedean Ammous, Jason A. Williams, Vijay Boyapati and Michael J. Saylor for your profound insights into Bitcoin.

To Satoshi Nakamoto wherever you are, Thank you.

Disclaimer

The content in this book is intended to provide general information on Bitcoin and is not to be taken as financial advice.

To learn more, please visit <u>bitcoin.org</u>

References

Quotes

1 - *"History has shown that governments will inevitably succumb to the temptation of inflating the money supply."*

Saifedean Ammous, Author, The Bitcoin Standard: The decentralized alternative to central banking, Page 67.

2 - *"The current financial system runs on printed cash. They are screwing with the money and it's hurting you and your family. That's why people buy bitcoin."*

Jason A. Williams, Author, Bitcoin: Hard Money You Can't F*ck With, Page 63.

3 - *"Right. Otherwise we couldn't have a finite limit of 21 million coins, because there would always need to be some minimum reward for generating. In a few decades when the reward gets too small, the transaction fee will become the main compensation for nodes. I'm sure that in 20 years there will either be very large transaction volume or no volume."*

**Satoshi Nakamoto February 14, 2010 bitcointalk.org.
https://bitcointalk.org/index.phptopic=48.msg329#msg329**

4 - *"Finally, fiat currencies, while only a relatively recent historical invention, have proven to be prone to constant increases in supply. Nation-states have shown a persistent proclivity to inflate their money supply to solve short-term political problems. The inflationary tendencies of governments across the world leave the owner of a fiat currency with the likelihood that their savings will diminish in value over time."*

Vijay Boyapati, Author, The Bullish Case for Bitcoin, Page 26.

5 - *"Bitcoin is a swarm of cyber hornets serving the goddess of wisdom, feeding on the fire of truth, exponentially growing ever smarter, faster, and stronger behind a wall of encrypted energy."*

Michael J. Saylor, co founder of MicroStrategy.
https://twitter.com/saylor/status/1307029562321231873?lang=en

Media

Lightning Logo on Lightning Network page supplied from:
https://commons.wikimedia.org/wiki/File:Bitcoin_lightning_logo.svg